WRITE RIGHT!

Writing
RESEARCH PAPERS

By Benjamin Proudfit

Gareth Stevens
PUBLISHING

Please visit our website, www.garethstevens.com. For a free color catalog of all our high-quality books, call toll free 1-800-542-2595 or fax 1-877-542-2596.

Library of Congress Cataloging-in-Publication Data

Proudfit, Benjamin.
Writing research papers / by Benjamin Proudfit.
p. cm. – (Write right!)
Includes index.
ISBN 978-1-4824-1121-8 (pbk.)
ISBN 978-1-4824-1122-5 (6-pack)
ISBN 978-1-4824-1120-1 (library binding)
1. Report writing – Juvenile literature. 2. Research – Juvenile literature. I. Title.
LB1047.3 P76 2015
808–d23

First Edition

Published in 2015 by
Gareth Stevens Publishing
111 East 14th Street, Suite 349
New York, NY 10003

Copyright © 2015 Gareth Stevens Publishing

Designer: Sarah Liddell
Editor: Kristen Rajczak

Photo credits: Cover, p. 1 Jupiterimages/Stockbyte/Thinkstock.com; p. 5 Olesya Feketa/Shutterstock.com; p. 7 Jiri Hera/Shutterstock.com; pp. 9, 19 Ingram Publishing/Thinkstock.com; p. 11 (index card) Chimpinski/iStock/Thinkstock.com; p. 11 (background) c8501089/iStock/Thinkstock.com; p. 13 Pressmaster/Shutterstock.com; p. 15 Jupiterimages/Goodshoot/Thinkstock.com; p. 17 (hurricane) Ablestock.com/Ablestock.com/Thinkstock.com; p. 17 (main) Flying Colours Ltd/Photodisc/Thinkstock.com; p. 21 (background) mexrix/Shutterstock.com; p. 21 (girl) Matthias G. Ziegler/Shutterstock.com.

Printed in the United States of America

CPSIA compliance information: Batch #CS15GS: For further information contact Gareth Stevens, New York, New York at 1-800-542-2595.

CONTENTS

Words in the glossary appear in **bold** type the first time they are used in the text.

LEARN SOMETHING NEW!

What do you know about Mars? What about Africa? Or the history of airplanes? There are so many **topics** to learn about all around us! A research paper gives you the chance to find out more about something you don't know much about. Research is the act of studying to find something new.

Research papers are common school **assignments**. They're commonly a longer piece of writing than an essay and have a few extra steps. These steps have to do with finding and using **sources**.

ON THE WRITE TRACK

Be sure to read your assignment carefully. Your teacher likely included how long the paper should be and how many sources you should use. To get the best grade, you'll want to follow all the directions given.

Writing a research paper is more than schoolwork. It's a way to dive into a topic you're not familiar with—yet!

THE TOPIC

Sometimes your teacher will give you a list of topics you may write your research paper about. In other cases, you may be allowed to choose your own topic. Either way, choose to write about something you find interesting or that you want to learn more about.

Next, narrow your topic. A general topic, such as hurricanes, will produce much more research than you need! It's easier to do research on a topic if you come up with a **specific** question about it to direct your research.

ON THE WRITE TRACK

If you're choosing your own topic, spend a few minutes writing down subjects that you're interested in, such as space, the rainforest, or monster trucks. Choose the topic that you think best fits the assignment.

Here are some examples of specific questions that can be asked about hurricanes. One of these could be the topic of a research paper.

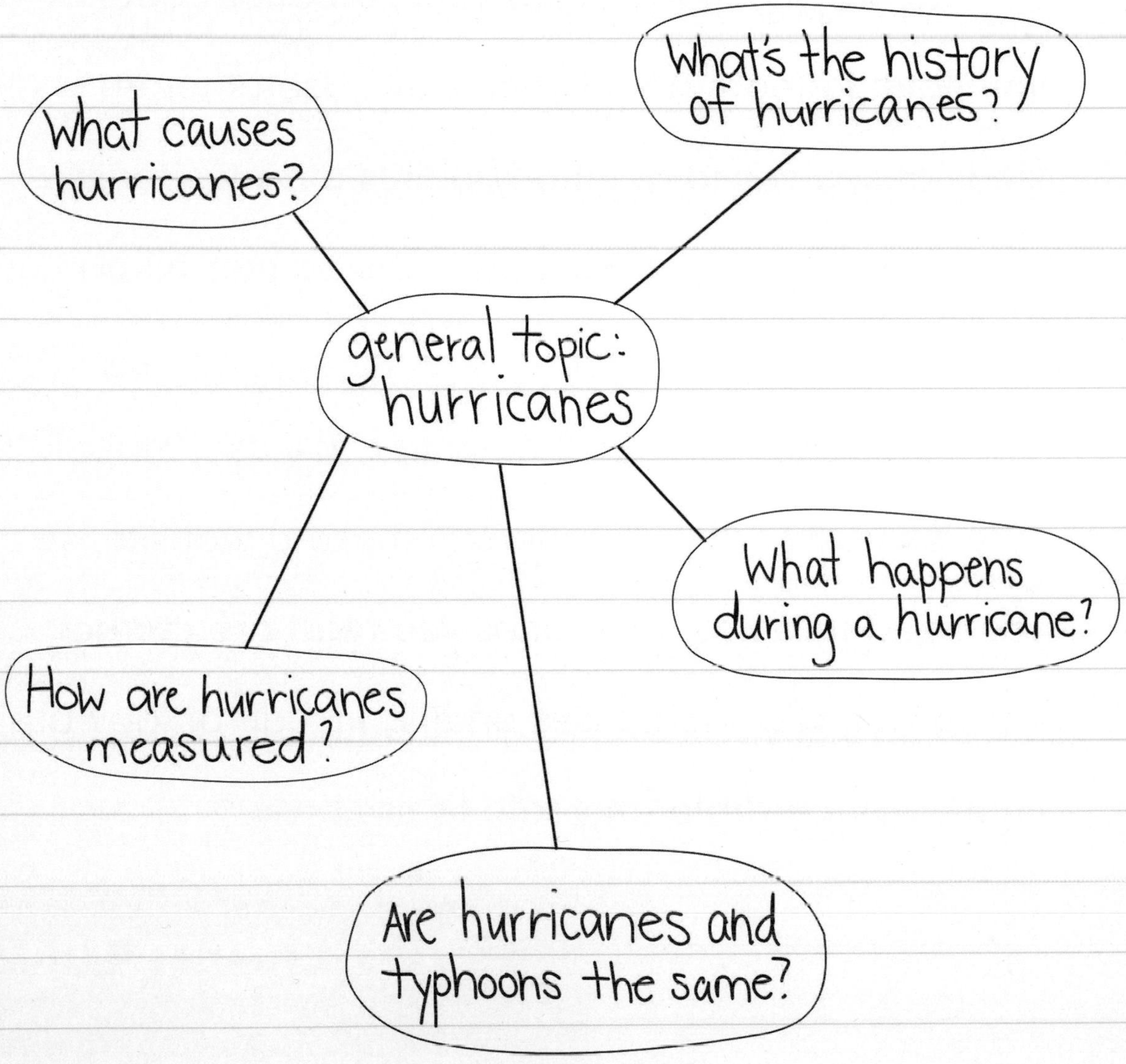

START YOUR RESEARCH

Before you start writing your research paper, you have to learn about your topic. Use different kinds of sources to get many points of view. Books, magazines, newspapers, and websites can all be used to find **information**.

No matter what kind of source you use, make sure it's trustworthy. Anyone can make a website, so you need to be sure the ones you read are correct. Those with web addresses ending in .edu or .gov are commonly **credible** and safe to use.

ON THE WRITE TRACK

Magazines and newspapers often print pieces that are based on opinions. These can still be helpful, but you need to be sure that the writer has backed up their opinion with facts.

The library is a good place to start your research. There, you can ask a librarian where to find the best books on your subject or use the electronic card catalog to find books on your own.

MAKE A PLAN

Once you've gathered enough sources, start to read through them. As you go, make notes about each. You can use a note card to write down facts you may use from each source, as the example on the next page shows.

An outline is the road map for your research paper. It lists your main points and the examples you've found in your research to support them. An outline can be as **detailed** as you want, or it could just be a few words about each idea.

ON THE WRITE TRACK

Think of your outline like a skeleton—it's just the bony structure to write from. Your sentences and ideas will be the flesh that brings the paper to life.

Be sure to note which source the information on each note card comes from.

http://www.nationalgeographic.com/features/04/forcesofnature/forces/hurricanes.html

-hurricanes are tropical storms with winds of at least 74 miles (119 km) per hour

-hurricanes are called cyclones and typhoons in other parts of the world

- most weather conditions that could cause a hurricane don't

-hurricanes have three parts: the eye, the eye wall, feeder bands

HOOK THE READER

The three parts of a research paper are the same as other writing assignments—an introduction, body, and conclusion.

In longer writing assignments like research papers, the introduction will be its own **paragraph**. The introduction tries to catch your reader's attention and lets your reader know what the paper will be about. The last sentence of your introduction will be your main topic sentence. Every point you make in your paper should support, or hold up, your main topic sentence.

ON THE WRITE TRACK

The "hook" of your introduction, or the part used to grab attention, can be a cool fact or **quote** you've found while researching your topic.

Even though it's first in the paper, the introduction doesn't have to be the first thing you write. Some people even find it easier to write the introduction last!

13

YOUR OWN WORDS

Before you start to write the body of your paper, keep in mind how you're going to use your sources. It's perfectly fine to use information from your source as long as you have put it into your own words, or paraphrased it. Here's an example using facts from *National Geographic*.

National Geographic: "About a hundred tropical disturbances develop every year, but less than 10 percent lead to anything but thunderstorms."

Paraphrased: Most of the weather conditions that could lead to hurricanes each year become nothing more than thunderstorms.

ON THE WRITE TRACK

Using someone else's work and saying it's your own is called plagiarism (PLAY-juh-rih-zuhm). It's a serious issue and should be avoided. In colleges, students who plagiarize may be thrown out of school.

If a source gives information in a particularly good way, you can use a quote. Put quotation marks (" ") around the words that you copy exactly from your source. Also, tell the reader where the quote is from, saying "according to" or "as reported by."

15

IN THE MIDDLE

The body of your research paper may be one paragraph or more. Each paragraph starts with a topic sentence that states the point of the paragraph. Then, examples and facts from your sources that support this statement should follow.

"Hurricane" is only one word of several used for a certain kind of storm. No matter where they happen, scientists call these storms tropical cyclones. In the Atlantic Ocean and northeast Pacific Ocean, they're called hurricanes. Cyclones are the same kind of storm but occur in the South Pacific Ocean and Indian Ocean. The word "typhoon" is used for this storm in the northwest Pacific Ocean.

ON THE WRITE TRACK

The conclusion is the last paragraph of your research paper. You'll use a few sentences to sum up the main points of your paper. No other specific examples are needed in the conclusion.

17

BIBLIOGRAPHY

At the end of your research paper, you should include a bibliography (bih-blee-AH-gruh-fee). This is a list of the sources you used. The bibliography gives credit to the places you found information. It also helps someone looking to learn more find sources quickly.

There are many ways to cite, or give information, about a source. You'll commonly include:

- the author's name
- the title of the book, article, or website
- the publisher
- where it was published or the web address
- the date it was published

ON THE WRITE TRACK

The easiest way to construct a bibliography is to keep track of the sources you use as you go along.

Bibliographies are always listed in alphabetical order by the author's last name. Sources that don't have an author, such as an encyclopedia, are included alphabetically by title.

19

PROOFREAD

Once you've written a draft of your paper, read through it. Check it against your assignment to make sure you've included all the parts and information you need to. Look for any errors or places that could be clearer. Then, make any changes you need to. This is called revision.

Are you happy with your paper? Make sure you have a copy with no marks left from revising your paper. Put your name at the top, and be proud of your hard work as you turn it in!

ON THE WRITE TRACK

A draft is an early attempt at something. Often, the first try at writing a paper is called the rough draft.

SAMPLE RESEARCH OUTLINE

1. introduction, topic sentence
2. body paragraph, main point 1
   a. example 1
   b. example 2
   c. example 3
3. body paragraph, main point 2
   a. example 1
   b. example 2
   c. example 3
4. body paragraph, main point 3
   a. example 1
   b. example 2
5. conclusion

GLOSSARY

assignment: a task or amount of work given to do

credible: reliable, believable

detailed: having lots of small parts

information: knowledge obtained from study or observation

paragraph: a group of sentences having to do with one idea or topic

quote: something that uses someone's exact words

source: a supplier of information

specific: clearly stated

topic: the subject or main idea of a paper

FOR MORE INFORMATION

BOOKS

Bodden, Valerie. *Writing a Research Paper*. Mankato, MN: Creative Education, 2014.

Manushkin, Fran. *Stick to the Facts, Katie: Writing a Research Paper with Katie Woo*. North Mankato, MN: Picture Window Books, 2014.

WEBSITES

Writing a Paper
kidshealth.org/teen/school_jobs/school/writing_papers.html
Learn more tips for writing successful school papers on this website for kids.

Writing Workshop: Research Paper
teacher.scholastic.com/activities/writing/index. asp?topic=Research
Follow this interactive guide when writing a research paper.

INDEX